Finding Daylight

Finding Daylight

How The Lord Works Through Our Disappointments

Kimberly Webb

LEATHERWOOD
PRESS

Leatherwood Press books are available exclusively
through Deseret Book Wholesale.

For details write or telephone
Deseret Book Wholesale, 40 East South Temple
Salt Lake City, Utah 84111, (801) 534-1515

Leatherwood Press LLC
8160 South Highland Drive
Sandy, Utah 84093
www.leatherwoodpress.com

Printed in the United States of America

Contents

.

Introduction

When life storms arise, clouding out the sun-light and filling me with gloom, I sense the Savior approaching. He is walking upon the violent waves, coming to my rescue. Do I hear my name on the wind? Yes, through the pelting rain He is calling to me, bidding me to come toward Him.

We all sometimes find ourselves upon figurative tempest-tossed seas, disoriented and in darkness. We long for daylight, or at the very least, an assuring voice to be our guide. Jesus Christ, the source of all comfort and light, calls to us. Will we step out of the boat? Will we choose to leave the darkness behind and step toward Him?

At times my answer is a frightened "no." Logically I believe that the voice calling to me belongs to an omnipotent, loving Redeemer; mentally I know He desires my peace and safety more than I do. But in my heart, I fear. I reflect on my past failures. I doubt I can walk on water because I've sunk so many times before.

A few years ago, I was sitting in my office at work when a distinct impression came to me: "You will be Relief Society president." I was new to the ward, and the revelation startled me. I determined to find out each sister's name and try to get to know the women better before they were asked to sustain me. A few weeks later, the Relief Society presidency was changed—but I was not called. I tossed aside my commitment to become involved in the ward and get to know each sister.

One year later the bishop called me into his office. "I feel impressed to call you as the Relief Society president," he said. My jaw dropped. I accepted the calling, but not without a slight feeling of shame—I knew few more sisters than I had the year before, even though

the Spirit had given me plenty of warning. How could I hear and obey promptings regarding this new weighty stewardship when I had doubted and ignored such promptings before? During the week between my call and sustaining, I was burdened by dark feelings of impending failure. Only fervent prayer, temple attendance, and priesthood blessings instilled hope in my heart that I could step out of the boat and try walking on water once more, if only I kept my eyes focused on the One who had called me.

I know I'm not alone in my fears. Whether the Savior invites us to accept a calling, improve a relationship, change direction in our lives, or set new goals, dwelling on past failings can hinder our progress. As mortals, we are prone to reviewing our experiences "through a glass, darkly" (1 Corinthians 13:12), perceiving many of our endeavors as unsuccessful. We may blame ourselves for imperfect outcomes or believe ourselves to be incompetent. The more displeased we are with our efforts, the less we feel capable of pleasing the Lord, and the less inclined we

are to step toward Him when He calls. As we cling to our failures, we lose faith in His desire to rescue us from the storm. We choose instead to drift further into the night.

At such times, there is another image that often comes to my mind—the brazen serpent in the wilderness, a symbol of Christ and His infinite healing power. As Moses raised the serpent, the Savior offered the obedient Israelites instant healing from their poisonous wounds. All they had to do was look. But sadly, Alma explains, "There were many who were so hardened that they would not look, therefore they perished" (Alma 33:20).

I used to think that those who were "hardened" refused to believe in anything illogical. They didn't believe an inanimate symbol could counter the natural consequences of a lethal snakebite, so they didn't bother to try. However, I believe Alma's plain explanation may refer to another type of hard-heartedness, one Church members are more likely to suffer: "Now the reason they would not look is because they did

not believe that it *would* heal them" (Alma 33:20, emphasis added). The word that strikes me is *would*—not *could*. The afflicted children of Israel may have had full confidence in God's healing ability, but they had no faith that He would heal *them*. They were haunted and hardened by past difficulties, perhaps blaming God or condemning themselves for bitter failures. They doubted either the Lord's love for them or their own worthiness to receive it. Focusing on negative past experiences, they put themselves out of His reach.

Heavenly Father and Jesus Christ do not withhold healing light, but sometimes we become too "hardened"—especially hard on ourselves—to accept it. When caught in the darkness of disappointment, little do we remember the true nature of so many mortal failings. They can be stepping-stones put in place by a loving God, pointing toward future success. They provide perfecting exercises in faith and patience, and they offer opportunities to repent and become new. Sometimes failure is the blessing itself as we are privileged to make sacrifices. No matter

the reason, some failure is necessary. Never slipping, sinking, nor fumbling on earth was Lucifer's plan. We chose the Lord's.

Daybreak awaits as we come to observe our failures in a new light—the merciful, instructive light of God. May we draw closer to Him in the process, accepting His extended, rescuing hand.

Chapter 1

Stepping-Stones: When Failure Points the Way

*H*eavenly Father speaks to His individual children in unique ways—through quiet whisperings, peaceful feelings, even music or the beauties of nature. I discovered early on that I understand the Spirit's instructions most clearly through holy words on a page. For me, nothing dispels the fog of confusion faster than kneeling to pray about a problem or a question, and then opening my scriptures to read. I know I'll always find peace and often a distinct answer. Nothing fills my soul with more joy than sensing my Father communicating with me in this way.

These treasured heavenly messages often come in response to my pleadings for solutions. Every now

and then, the Lord powerfully answers questions I have not yet asked.

The Lord's Formula for Success

While reading 1 Nephi chapters 3 and 4, the account of Nephi striving to obtain the brass plates from Laban, I remember coming across a quote by a Church leader in my study guide. He explained that the attempt to get the plates is illustrative of every mortal's natural approach to solving problems. First, he pointed out, Nephi's brother Laman went into Laban's house and talked to Laban. Laman's first instinct was to rely upon his own intellect and powers of persuasion. When that attempt failed, the brothers devised a second plan to try to buy the plates from Laban, choosing to rely on material resources. This plan also failed. Only when Nephi submitted to the Lord's way—by following the Spirit—did God deliver the plates. So it is with us. When we sacrifice our natural securities, submit ourselves to the Lord's will, and commit to follow His guid-

ance at all costs, He will prepare the way for us to obey His commandments, and He will deliver every good thing into our lives.

I liked the quote and remember taking meticulous notes in my scripture journal.

A few days later my mom said, "Listen to this great lesson I learned in my scripture study." She started explaining her insight, which was exactly like the quote I had written down.

I excitedly interrupted and finished what she was going to say. "We must be reading the same study guide," I said.

She looked confused. "I didn't read it in a book. This is something the Spirit taught me."

I couldn't believe she had coincidentally quoted a General Authority. I wanted to show her the quote, but when I opened my scripture journal to where I had left off, I found nothing recorded for 1 Nephi chapters 3 and 4. "Maybe I didn't write it down," I murmured, but I knew that wasn't true. I reviewed

the study guide, sensing something strange happening. Nothing there looked familiar either.

Slowly I accepted that I had never read such a quote. The Lord was trying to get my attention. He wanted me to listen so closely that He had placed a memory in my mind, perhaps through a dream, that never really happened.

The Test

Soon afterwards I received an unexpected impression to move so I could increase my spiritual and social growth. I assumed moving closer to my job would be a bonus. I found an apartment inside a house I liked because it was quaint, five minutes away from work, and occupied by a roommate with similar hobbies and a contagious enthusiasm. The apartment was more expensive than I had hoped and I wasn't sure about the area of town, but remembering my recent lesson from Nephi, I decided not to worry too much about my own rationale or material means. I prayed for guidance and felt nothing amiss. A few weeks later I moved in.

As long as my roommate Rachael was around, I felt at home. Unfortunately, that feeling lasted only a day. The next day she and her family, who lived in the apartment next door, left on a two-week vacation. Suddenly the quaint old house became spooky. I hadn't noticed until now that Rachael hadn't had time to buy blinds yet. No matter where I was inside, an empty window glared at me through flimsy transparent curtains.

That night I decided to go outside for some fresh air. As soon as I stepped through the dark entryway onto my porch, a feeling of urgency swallowed me. A voice spoke to my mind: *Get back into your apartment before someone else does.* I flew through the dark entryway back inside and locked the door. No sooner had I done so than the doorknob—ever so silently—twisted back and forth. My stomach went cold. Someone had been nearby watching me! He had stealthily tried to follow me inside. Without thinking, I punched the weak wooden door with my fist, an unspoken warning. I never saw nor heard him, but I sensed when the threat had passed. I wearily sank to the floor.

The next day my ever-inspired mom told me she had known I was in danger. Picturing a man hiding in my entryway, she had prayed for my safety through the night. My decision was made. I packed up and left. Rachael understood that I couldn't live in a place where I wasn't safe when she and her family were gone.

I was beyond grateful for the Lord's protection that night, but I was also confused. Hadn't He given me the lesson from Nephi at that particular time for a reason—to help me move where He wanted me to be? I had done my best to follow the pattern. I thought I had followed the Spirit, yet I had failed to find a good, safe place. I was obviously no better than Laman, still relying too heavily on my own logic and nearly getting myself killed as a result!

Purposeful Dead Ends

Failing while sincerely trying to obey can introduce helpless feelings. We can be tempted to avoid seeking further promptings, not trusting our ability to interpret them.

Elder Jeffrey R. Holland's son Matt faced a similarly perplexing problem as a 12-year-old boy: "Returning from an exploring trip on backcountry roads, he and his father came to an unexpected fork and could not remember which road to take. It was late in the day, and they knew darkness would be enveloping them in unfamiliar territory. Seizing a teaching moment, Jeffrey Holland asked his son to pray for direction. Afterward, he asked his son what he felt, and Matt replied that he felt strongly they should go to the left. Replying that he had felt the same way, his father turned the truck to the left. Ten minutes later, they came to a dead end and returned to take the other route.

"Matt thought for a time and then asked his father why they would get that kind of answer to a prayer. His father replied that with the sun going down, that was undoubtedly the quickest way for the Lord to give them information—in this case, which one was the wrong road. Now, though the other road might not be familiar and could be difficult in places, they

could proceed confidently, knowing it was the right one, even in the dark" (Don L. Searle, "Elder Jeffrey R. Holland of the Quorum of the Twelve Apostles," *Ensign*, Dec. 1994, 10).

I believe Matt Holland's experience holds meaning for us all. The Lord likewise communicates with us, at times providing information through purposeful dead ends. At these times we must prayerfully seek the other fork in the road. We may gain courage by revisiting 1 Nephi 3 and 4.

Success in Steps

Like many of us, Nephi was striving to obey a personal commandment when he experienced failure. Plan A to retrieve the plates hadn't worked. Plan B, the idea to buy the plates, did not come from slothful, shortsighted Laman or Lemuel—it came from Nephi. As he made the suggestion, he faithfully testified: "As the Lord liveth, and as we live, we will not go down unto our father in the wilderness until we have accomplished the thing which the Lord hath commanded us. . . .

"And behold, it is wisdom in God that we should obtain these records, that we may preserve unto our children the language of our forefathers;

"And also that we may preserve unto them the words which have been spoken by the mouth of all the holy prophets" (1 Nephi 3:15, 19–20).

This does not sound like a person refusing the guidance of the Holy Ghost! In fact, Nephi's great faith is evident in his reasons for getting the plates in the first place. Yes, he was motivated by obedience to the Lord's commandments, but he also felt an urgent need to preserve records for his *children.* At this time, Nephi was heading into the wilderness with only his family, no marriage prospects in sight. His faith gave him the assurance that he would yet be blessed with posterity.

I believe that, in faith, Nephi probably felt he was following the Spirit all along. He may have assumed the idea to buy the plates was inspired, just as I felt my plan to move into Rachael's house was inspired. Yet when the plan failed, Nephi did not wallow in a

feeling of failure, as I had. He did not feel betrayed by the Lord nor his own feelings. Unlike his brothers, he refused to give up.

The writer Elbert Hubbard could have been describing the contrast between Nephi's response and so many of ours when he said: "Genius is only the power of making continuous efforts. The line between failure and success is so fine that we scarcely know when we pass it: so fine that we are often on the line and do not know it. How many a man has thrown up his hands at a time when a little more effort, a little more patience, would have achieved success. . . . A little more persistence, a little more effort, and what seemed hopeless failure may turn to glorious success. There is no failure except in no longer trying. There is no defeat except from within, no really insurmountable barrier save our own inherent weakness of purpose." (*Light from Many Lamps*, edited by Lillian Eichler Watson, New York: Simon & Schuster, 1979, 152).

Nephi's purpose was firm. He was inspired by eternal perspective, and this noble motive finally

drove him to the line between success and failure. That line is very definite in our modern-day perspective but was perhaps imperceptible to Nephi as he approached Laban lying unconscious in the street. Elder Holland once pointed out, "How much is hanging in the balance as Nephi stands over the drunken Laban I cannot say, but it is a great deal indeed. The dramatic irony here is that we know what a pivotal moment this is, but Nephi may not. And regardless of how much is at stake, how can he do this thing? He is a good person, perhaps even a well-educated person. He has been taught from the very summit of Sinai, 'Thou shalt not kill.' And he has made gospel covenants" (*On Earth as It Is in Heaven*, Deseret Book, 1989, 129). How wrenching the prompting to kill Laban must have been! What a counterintuitive solution! No wonder Nephi "shrank and would that [he] might not slay [Laban]" (1 Nephi 4:10).

As Nephi stood deliberating, an interesting sequence of thoughts unfolded in his mind, communicated by the Holy Ghost: "And the Spirit said unto

me again: Behold the Lord hath delivered him into thy hands. Yea, and I also knew that he had sought to take away mine own life; yea, and he would not hearken unto the commandments of the Lord; and he also had taken away our property" (v. 11). How did Nephi know that Laban would not hearken unto the commandments of the Lord? Because Laman had gone into Laban's house and talked to him, asking for the plates. Laban had not hearkened. How could Nephi say that Laban was a murderer and a thief? Laban had stolen Nephi's goods and had twice sent guards to kill him and his brothers.

What seemed like failed attempts in Nephi's experience were stepping-stones; they boosted Nephi's confidence when the difficult instruction came. Surely Nephi was faithful enough to follow the Spirit under any circumstances, but the Lord knew Nephi's pure heart. He understood the doubt Nephi would feel in carrying out such a repulsive command. In His mercy, the Lord allowed Laban to acquire incriminating evidence against himself first. He permitted Nephi

to fail and hence to know by his own experience that Laban was unbending—that there was no other way. "Therefore I did obey the voice of the Spirit," Nephi records (1 Nephi 4:18). He obtained the plates and preserved the faith of generations.

Our Own Stepping-Stones

I recognize that my attempts to find a new home hardly compare with the sacrifice required of Nephi. Neither do greater failures in most of our lives come close to the frustration Nephi may have felt before succeeding in fulfilling such a crucial command. Yet I sensed the Holy Ghost communicating applicable truths to me through this account. A burden lifted as I realized I had not failed the Lord in choosing a poor place to live. He understood my pure desire to follow Him, but He also knew my limited understanding. The right answer would be counterintuitive, something I would not come to on my own without small guiding steps.

As we face dead ends, we are given a blessing—the wonderful opportunity to cast away preconceived

assumptions. We can proceed with confidence when the right solution comes, no longer hesitating when it contradicts what we may have expected.

Three months later I moved to a city 25 miles south from where I had initially been willing to consider. I'm grateful I did. The Lord knew where I could serve the best, feel the safest, and meet influential people in my life.

After learning from Nephi's experience, I reflected on other instances when I had been guided through failure. For years I had tried to pursue talents in art, at first majoring in illustration. It took a few disappointments before I settled for using my most natural gift of writing. Little did I know I was not "settling" for failure in other fields; I was developing the gift Heavenly Father wanted me to use most.

Seeing past failures in this light can turn our sense of inadequacy into profound gratitude. Truly God sometimes hedges up the way to lovingly redirect our course. Elder Richard G. Scott once said: "Most often

what we have chosen to do is right. He will confirm the correctness of our choices His way. That confirmation generally comes through packets of help found along the way. We discover them by being spiritually sensitive. They are like notes from a loving Father as evidence of His approval. If, in trust, we begin something which is not right, He will let us know before we have gone too far" ("Learning to Recognize Answers to Prayer," *Ensign*, Nov. 1989, 30). Sometimes the way He lets us know is through failure. We can come to see such disappointments as another type of "help packet," one that points out the path in an unexpected way.

Now when I face failures, I try to remember that perhaps I have not failed; the story is unfinished. For each of us, glorious successes await on the other side of defeat. At times there is simply no other way to reach them but to follow the stepping-stones.

Chapter 2

Awaiting the Harvest: When Success is Delayed

The summer before my sophomore year of high school, I decided to join the cross-country team. In my small town try-outs were not required and I felt confident I could eventually earn a spot on the varsity team. I got up bright and early one morning, put on some headphones, and bounded out the door. A half-mile later, I'd had enough. I wasn't too worried because I figured I had all summer to build up to three miles.

When school started I learned that running a 5K race competitively requires training at much longer distances. I was the worst runner on the team. Determined to catch up, I threw myself into training, but by

the weekend my nose started bleeding and wouldn't stop. Three hours later, a doctor cauterized the vessels and instructed me to avoid running that week. The next week my wisdom teeth came out and I was back on the couch. By the time I was well enough to compete, I was even slower than before.

I longed to improve at the upcoming home meet. I hoped that, like a legendary Olympic athlete, the strength of my determination could somehow override physical setbacks. Maybe I could even make the top eight, varsity level.

The morning of the race I woke up with a jaw the size of a golf ball. I needed to be put under general anesthesia again, the doctor explained, while he opened the sore and treated the infection. Tears rolled down my face as the nurse administered the shot. I knew I'd never recover from another surgery in time. My coach insisted I stay home during the next two meets and run at the regional championship, but everyone knew I didn't stand a chance of qualifying for state. Thus ended my first and only cross-country season.

My grandpa had been a marathon runner, but I decided I must not have gotten any of his genes. I wasn't the kind of person who could run insane distances despite all odds. One of my teammates had even accused me of being a wimp. Maybe he was right. I had failed to improve my time by even one minute.

Ten years later, I barreled toward mile 10 in the Moab Half Marathon. A crowd of percussionists pounded away near the trail, celebrating our approach to the finish line. The rows of performers, the bright blue sky, the striking red rock, and thousands of determined runners blended into surreal beauty. I had to swallow the lump in my throat to keep my pace.

As I raced along the Colorado River, I reflected on my first attempt at running a mere half-mile. I remembered my cross-country coach's patience and my teammate's skepticism. Most of all, I remembered my grandpa. He had recently passed away, but I felt him near as I ran. Maybe we had more in common than I originally thought.

When I crossed the finish line, I finally felt the success I had longed for as an awkward 15-year-old.

Sowing Seeds

By almost any serious runner's standards, my cross-country season was an embarrassment. But when I decided to train for a half marathon, I discovered valuable seeds I had planted back then, such as the capacity to mentally focus and endure. I knew how to conserve energy and when to spend it. I knew the best stretches, and I knew which shoes would help keep my weak ankles steady. Most of all, I better understood the level of training and commitment that would be required. As a self-conscious teen I had been too consumed with my failings to notice what I had gained.

Every time we embark upon something new, we plant a seed. Sometimes we may plant many seeds. Matthew 13:4–8 reads: "And when he sowed, some seeds fell by the way side, and the fowls came and devoured them up:

"Some fell upon stony places, where they had not much earth: and forthwith they sprung up, because they had no deepness of earth:

"And when the sun was up, they were scorched; and because they had no root, they withered away.

"And some fell among thorns; and the thorns sprung up, and choked them:

"But other fell into good ground, and brought forth fruit, some an hundredfold, some sixtyfold, some thirtyfold."

Like the sower described in the parable, we may cast many seeds upon unfavorable ground before one bears fruit. Brent A. Barlow comments, "The parable was originally given in regard to the people's receptivity to the message of Jesus Christ. But there is another significant message contained in the parable: not everything we attempt to do in life is going to be successful; every seed we sow will not necessarily take root" (*Just for Newlyweds*, Deseret Book, 1992, 123).

We can do everything possible to plant seeds in what appears to be favorable ground. As a healthy teen, I saw no reason why I could not be successful in running. But at that particular time, my goal was "choked "with "thorns" I hadn't foreseen.

Sometimes the circumstances for achieving goals are ideal—the ground is good—but we still don't succeed. Alma 32:32 reads, "Therefore, if a seed groweth it is good, *but if it groweth not, behold it is not good*, therefore it is cast away" (emphasis added). The goal itself may not be good for us. Obviously we will receive no divine help in pursuing unworthy goals, but even when we work toward righteous, worthwhile objectives, we cannot know with certainty what our efforts will yield. We cannot always know which seeds are good for us specifically.

Nurturing in Faith

So what is the point of working to nurture so many seeds if Heavenly Father already knows which ones are good? Can't He tell us which goals to pursue be-

fore we bother risking failure? Sometimes we may receive impressions directing us in a straight course to success, but most of the time we plant, nurture, and face uncertainty. Doubt and pessimism are the opposites of faith, but *uncertainty* doesn't always reflect doubt. Were that the case, none of us could exercise faith during this very uncertain mortal existence.

I discovered this principle as a ward missionary. I made a dinner appointment with the full-time missionaries, then prayed to find someone to invite. Nothing seemed to pan out. Finally I decided to make loaves of pumpkin bread and venture into the neighborhood, hoping to randomly meet someone new. I knew the Lord would be pleased with my desire to serve, but I also felt a twinge of uncertainty. I worried that He would deny me success because I could not sense *for sure* if my approach was right.

In my scripture journal entry for Alma 32:21 I had written: "Faith is how we know things spiritually before we have solid physical evidence. Having faith in something doesn't mean we are any less

certain—it just means we 'know' it in a different dimension than we 'know' other things." The oft-quoted Bible Dictionary likewise affirms that true faith "carries an assurance of the fulfillment of things hoped for" (Bible Dictionary, "Faith," 670). For example, we may know with certainty that our souls have eternal worth long before we enter the eternities. We may know that the Book of Mormon is true even though we cannot prove it to the satisfaction of secular people. At times, we may know by revelation matters of personal importance, such as which career to pursue, whom to marry, or where to live. The Spirit can move upon us so powerfully that we can honestly say we "know" something before the tangible evidence arrives.

However, in focusing on the strong assurance that comes of mature faith in some areas, we cannot undervalue the small beginnings of new faith in other areas. Alma calls these beginnings a desire to believe, or in other words, *a willingness to find out*. He explains that we *cannot* know with certainty until *after* we have

experimented (see Alma 32:26–27). Spiritual and physical evidence combined create a "perfect knowledge" (Alma 32:21), and we can't expect a nearly perfect knowledge based on spiritual evidence alone in every scenario we face. President Boyd K. Packer shared a related experience: "We once had a major decision to make. When our prayers left us uncertain, I went to see Elder Harold B. Lee. He counseled us to proceed. Sensing that I was still very unsettled, he said, 'The problem with you is you want to see the end from the beginning.' Then he quoted this verse from the Book of Mormon, 'Dispute not because ye see not, for ye receive no witness until after the trial of your faith' (Ether 12:6).

"He added, 'You must learn to walk a few steps ahead into the darkness, and then the light will turn on and go before you.' That was a life-changing experience" ("The Book of Mormon: Another Testament of Jesus Christ," *Ensign*, May 2005, 8).

Now I better understand that faith does not mean praying so hard that we can always sense Heavenly

Father telling us which seeds to plant or how or when. Most of the time, exercising faith means using our God-given agency to act despite uncertainty. Faith moves "its possessor to some kind of physical and mental action" (Bible Dictionary, "Faith," 670). Meanwhile, we can possess the "assurance of the fulfillment of things hoped for" if we ultimately hope for the Lord's will to occur in our lives. We can have this kind of faith even when we feel uncertain about our specific proximate hopes. Our sincere efforts to act, to exercise faith, can grant us a feeling of achievement regardless of the outcome.

Reaping the Harvest

Sometimes we plant seeds dealing with missionary work, as in my experience. I followed Alma's counsel and "experimented" with six loaves of bread that Sunday and befriended two families who shared dinner with the missionaries.

Even when our missionary efforts fail, we've planted seeds that may grow later. At age 14 my friend

Whitney underlined her favorite verses in a new copy of the Book of Mormon. She wrapped up the Christmas gift and gave it to our long-time friend Kristen, a self-proclaimed atheist. Kristen understood what the book meant to Whitney and appreciated the gesture, but she stashed it in her closet without intending to crack it open. Imagine Whitney's joy when, eight years later, she and I drove Kristen to the Salt Lake Temple to be married. As a young adult, Kristen had eventually dusted off Whitney's gift after all.

Sometimes the missionary seeds we plant are within ourselves more than in those we contact. I remember a time I felt impressed to speak to a woman I'd passed on the sidewalk. I caught up to her and asked, "Are you visiting Salt Lake?"

Her eyes lit up. "Yes," she said in a thick accent. "I'm lost. Can you direct me to the mall?"

I gave her directions and she bustled off. I stood there confused, wondering if I should have been more persistent.

The next day I decided to stroll around Temple Square before going to work. The missionaries had not yet arrived, and everything was still. I smiled at two people standing near the Tabernacle and felt the familiar nudge to talk to them. The two tourists, a mother and son, were from Austria. The missionaries would not arrive for another 30 minutes, so I offered to accompany them to the observation deck of the Church Office Building. I gave them copies of the German *Liahona* and, an hour later, walked them back to Temple Square where an Austrian missionary greeted them. I hugged my new friends goodbye and held onto the scrap of paper they had given me with their address on it. Later that year I traveled on business to Austria and passed on the referral.

Looking back, I see the moment I spoke to the woman at the crosswalk as a seed planted within myself—I nurtured a willingness to follow promptings and open my mouth. Had I not shown the Lord I

would obey such promptings, I may not have met my two Austrian friends the next day. Nurturing seeds that don't grow can be great preparation for reaping the harvest of good seeds.

The same principle is at work when we build new relationships. It's far too common for singles to fear dating seriously, trying to avoid getting hurt or hurting another person. Yet these experiences are necessary. Only through planting a seed—allowing ourselves to be vulnerable, show our hearts, and honestly view the heart of another—can we know if a seed is good. Only then will we discover if the relationship grows, if it begins to enlarge our soul and become delicious to us (see Alma 32:28).

We must also plant seeds in finding new talents, discovering our gifts, pursuing educational and professional goals, and seeking personal development in dozens of ways. I've sown more seeds than I can count that never really amounted to anything—piano lessons, viola lessons, baton twirling lessons, equestrian lessons, dance lessons, oil painting lessons—the

list could go on. But instead of numbering our many failed attempts, we can glory in the discovery of one or two seeds that flourish beautifully.

No matter the experiment, the promise is the same: if the seed is good, the ground is good, and our efforts sincere, the seed will grow and we will reap the harvest.

Patiently Waiting

Sometimes we fear we have failed when really we haven't waited long enough for results. My experience waiting 10 years to run a race successfully is one example; Whitney's success as a member missionary is another.

Ecclesiastes reminds us that there is an appointed length of time between planting and harvesting: "To every thing there is a season, and a time to every purpose under the heaven: . . . a time to plant, and a time to pluck up that which is planted" (3:1–2). This period of waiting presents the perfect opportunity to gain patience.

The virtue of patience is closely entwined with hope, one of the three greatest attributes we can achieve in mortality (see 1 Corinthians 13:13). Romans 8:25 explains what it means to hope: "But if we hope for that we see not, then do we *with patience wait* for it" (emphasis added). The definition of hope includes patience! In fact, the words "hope" and "wait" are described by the same verb in Spanish: *esperar*. We exert faith to plant a seed and nurture it, and then we exercise hope by patiently waiting to see it grow at its naturally appointed pace.

Elder Neal A. Maxwell described patience this way: "It is accepting a divine rhythm to life; it is obedience prolonged. Patience stoutly resists pulling up the daisies to see how the roots are doing!" ("Patience," *Ensign*, Oct. 1980, 30.)

It is difficult to be patient when the fulfillment of our hopes is at stake. It's hard to wait for time's natural processes, but patiently waiting ensures that we do not take matters into our hands that belong in the Lord's.

I think of the beautiful description in D&C 88:42–47: "He hath given a law unto all things, by which they move in their times and seasons;

"And their courses are fixed, even the courses of the heavens and the earth, which comprehend the earth and all the planets.

"And they give light to each other in their times and in their seasons, in their minutes, in their hours, in their days, in their weeks, in their months, in their years—all these are one year with God, but not with man.

"The earth rolls upon her wings, and the sun giveth his light by day, and the moon giveth her light by night, and the stars also give their light, as they roll upon their wings in their glory, in the midst of the power of God.

"Unto what shall I liken these kingdoms, that ye may understand?

"Behold, all these are kingdoms, and any man who hath seen any or the least of these hath seen

God moving in his majesty and power."

Can we remember that the Lord who sustains universes also upholds our own small world? He brings about changing seasons in our individual lives and prolongs needed experiences according to His perfect timing.

This section of scripture first touched me as I sat waiting in a temple chapel for my session to begin. My first time through the temple was a little confusing, and for the first three months after being endowed I attended weekly in order to gain a stronger testimony of temple ordinances. For two months I sensed little progress. Some days I enjoyed the simple peace of the temple although I didn't understand much of what was being taught. Other days I came home frustrated that I could not partake of the learning feast that so many had told me would be a part of my temple experience.

Then one afternoon I went to the temple fasting. I read D&C 88 while waiting and suddenly saw

personal meaning in the account of the Creation. I felt the Lord's hand in every aspect of my life and knew I had a place among His works. Through the entire session I felt the Holy Ghost near, opening my eyes and whispering insight after insight. To this day, most of what I understand about the temple endowment was given to me in those two pivotal hours.

How grateful I am that I waited for my testimony to grow, that I was patient with the Lord's timing for teaching me. He required that I sow seeds of obedience first, and at the appropriate time, they grew into knowledge. Had I decided prematurely that I was a failure at discerning symbolism, I may have ceased attending the temple as often and missed a treasured spiritual harvest.

Perhaps my favorite example of patience is found in the Book of Mormon. Abish, a Lamanite woman who secretly believed in the gospel, was serving in King Lamoni's household at the time of his miraculous conversion. How long Abish served there I do not know, but I try to envision how she must have

felt living the gospel alone before Ammon came onto the scene. Did she wish to bear her testimony but was prompted not to? Did she ever feel inadequate, unable to share what she knew?

I think of Abish toiling one seemingly unremarkable day after another. I wonder if she envisioned her capacity for influence when her opportunities seemed so limited. How many times do we feel less than remarkable, wishing to be better instruments in the Lord's hands rather than fulfill mundane daily tasks?

Yet by fulfilling her duties, Abish was in the right place to take advantage of a wonderful opportunity. When Ammon arrived and instigated a miraculous conversion among the royal household, it was the lowly servant Abish who ran from house to house, bringing a multitude to witness the works of God. She served as the linchpin in converting many, all because she patiently awaited the Lord's timing. She sowed a life of quiet dedication, filled with honorable work, and reaped missionary success in a dramatic way.

Seeking Growth

May we follow the example of the sower, refusing to give up when some seeds don't grow. We can exert constant effort, remembering faithful servants like Abish who eventually reaped grand rewards.

Only the Lord knows what we will eventually harvest—only He knows the good seeds in our lives. In the meantime, it is our job to nurture every seed in faith, resting assured that *we* will grow through our efforts.

Chapter 3

"The Darkness Is Past": When Failure Brings Change

I begin this chapter with a personally heart-wrenching experience I encountered a few years ago as a young adult in a new singles ward.

On one of my first days there, I heard a voice behind me say quietly, "Hey, Kim."

Startled, I turned to see Clete's timid smile and steady brown eyes. I waved but kept walking. *How does he know my name?* I wondered. Since I'd joined the singles ward two weeks ago, he hadn't said three words to me. I wasn't outgoing either—I'd be moving away in a few months, and I figured there was no use becoming attached.

Every week, Clete still looked me in the eye, smiled, and called me by name. I wasn't very friendly in return. *Maybe he has a crush on me*, I worried. *Or worse, maybe I'm his service project.* That was the last thing I needed.

At a fireside, Clete sat behind my younger brother Carl and me. He clapped Carl's back and asked, "How are you?"

Surprised, I whispered to Carl, "You know him?"

Carl shrugged. "Not really. But when I see him at the gym, he says hi anyway."

Sheepishly I recognized that Clete was kind to everyone.

A few weeks later, I volunteered at the family history center. When I arrived, Clete was talking to the service missionaries.

"Oh, good! You're here," Sister Thomas said. "Our other volunteers didn't come today, but we can always count on Clete to step in. He's been here for hours."

He stared at the floor, embarrassed. I was shocked! He had struck me as too quiet to readily volunteer. Obviously there was a lot I didn't know about Clete. My admiration for him was growing, but I still didn't have time to bother with new friends.

On my last day in the ward, Clete approached me. "Kim, please don't go," he said. He was gently teasing me, but his eyes were filled with genuine disappointment. I couldn't believe it—he'd miss me! I was flattered, but I shrugged it off. Without thanking him or telling him how much I admired his kindness, I said goodbye.

A few months later, Clete was killed in a car accident. Feeling sick, I remembered the last time I had seen him, the last time I had ignored the opportunity to be his friend.

At the funeral I learned who he really was. The person I had considered timid had recently performed in a university play! He was an Eagle Scout and a black belt in karate. Why hadn't I taken the

time to know these things about him? Most importantly, he had quietly served family, neighbors, and friends. He had tried to include me in that circle of friendship, but I had resisted. Now it was too late.

For weeks I worried and grieved. I wondered how often I underestimated people, failing to see their amazing gifts and welcome their influence into my life. I knew that I could never be perfect in my relationships with others, and that no matter how hard I tried, I would likely harbor regrets whenever someone passed away. But the depth of my mourning and guilt seemed more than typical. I knew I needed to repent.

Comfort finally came from a scripture: "The darkness is past; the true light now shineth" (1 John 2:8). As I read the calming words, I knew how to be healed. I couldn't change the past, but I could change. I could repent of the indifferent way I treated those around me. After weeks of unbearable pain, I felt the dark cloud lifting and the peaceful light of Christ shining through. I resolved to find joy in living the Christlike way that Clete had.

Wandering in the Wilderness

To put it bluntly, some amount of disappointment *is* our own fault, and this can be the hardest kind of failure to swallow. If only we'd known better—or done what we knew was right all along—the outcome could have been different.

I imagine the disappointment of those who marched with Zion's Camp. I think of Lehi's family, and, before him, hosts of Israelites wandering in the wilderness. Failure to make progress is often the price of disobedience; Zion's Camp could not redeem Zion, the Israelites were barred from the promised land for 40 years, and for eight years Lehi's family endured periods of time during which they "did not progress in their journey; . . . They tarried in the wilderness, or did not travel in a direct course" (Alma 37:42; see 1 Nephi 17:4).

We've all wasted time wandering when we could have been pressing forward, but we need not be yoked to such debt forever. For repentant souls,

the Lord paves a path toward possibilities eternally equal to those that were lost. Miraculously, Heavenly Father and Jesus Christ can even take the bitterness out of our past failures, just as He removed my grief and guilt for having forsaken the opportunity to be a good friend. In time, we may see our mistakes as sacred learning experiences —but only if we are willing to learn.

Growing Pains

As I discovered through mourning Clete's death, we can deal with mistakes in one of two ways. We can grit our teeth and survive until the pain subsides, leaving fear to fester in its place. With this approach, we never look upward or inward but continue wandering, dreading the next trial because we have not become more equipped to handle adversity. The other option is to change. We can examine our sin, experience the pain and regret fully, and allow God to heal us from the inside out. Then we don't worry as much about future trials because we have experienced Christ's

healing. We know from experience that He can heal us again.

The difference between changing rather than merely surviving lies in our willingness to be vulnerable. It lies in our courage to be honest with ourselves and ask Heavenly Father to show us our faults. He will respond, and we will never feel more loved. If we submit, He will ease the burden of our failures and grant us new opportunities. This kind of change both requires courage and increases it.

Joseph Smith stands as a great example of change. It took only one lapse in good judgment, allowing Martin Harris to take the 116 pages, for Joseph to commit full and constant obedience to the Lord. If only all of us were so humble! Elder Dallin H. Oaks of the Quorum of the Twelve Apostles stated, "As someone has said, there is a big difference between 20 years' experience and 1 year's experience repeated 20 times. If we understand the Lord's teachings and promises, we will learn and grow from our adversities" ("Give Thanks in All Things," *Ensign*, May

2003, 96). If we do not understand the Lord's teachings, we may be tempted to close our hearts to His tutoring, blame others, and deflect the lessons we could have learned.

The Lord mercifully strives to teach His children the lessons they need in order to become like Him. It's possible that similar, repeated failures reflect an unwillingness on our part to learn a vital principle. I've found that whenever I ever think, "Not *this* again," my trial evidences a loving Father's continued efforts to teach me.

Elder Bruce C. Hafen of the Seventy has explained that "there are growing pains that come from learning through our mistakes. Learning from our own errors requires that we honestly acknowledge them, something that is always painful for those who strive for competence" (*The Broken Heart*, Deseret Book, 1989, 86). Elder Neal A. Maxwell of the Quorum of the Twelve Apostles described one way such pain finds us: "If a sudden, stabbing light exposes the gap between what we are and what we

think we are, can we . . . let that light be a healing laser?" ("Irony: the Crust on the Bread of Adversity," *Ensign*, May 1989, 64).

The source of light is the Savior. His light reveals truth, and His light heals. We cannot receive one without the other. We must see the truth about ourselves, including our sins, if we are to be healed. We must honestly examine the cause of our failures before we can leave them behind.

Learning from Experience

Those who marched with Zion's Camp faced a "stabbing light" type of realization. As Church members, they believed in the Lord's promises regarding Zion and expected Him to grant them immediate success in reclaiming their stolen land from Missouri mobs. While they saw the truth about their identity (beloved, covenant members of the Lord's Church), they looked past the truth about some of the Saints' conduct. They had broken covenants and forfeited their claim on promised blessings.

We must strive to see the truth about ourselves, no matter how unflattering. If we are unwilling to see the whole truth in its glaring light, we can be tempted to blame God for our disappointments. He warns against this tendency: "Who am I, saith the Lord, that have promised and have not fulfilled?

"I command and men obey not; I revoke and they receive not the blessing.

"Then they say in their hearts: This is not the work of the Lord, for his promises are not fulfilled. But wo unto such, for their reward lurketh beneath and not from above" (D&C 58:31–33).

If we choose to accept the truth and grow, we can expect to sometimes hear the painful pronouncement given to the early Latter-day Saints echoing in our ears: "They have not learned to be obedient to the things which I required at their hands . . . And my people must needs be chastened until they learn obedience, if it must needs be, by the things which they suffer" (D&C 105:3, 6).

We can rest assured that we are living meaningful lives when suffering teaches and, ultimately, uplifts us. Elder Hafen pointed out, "If you have problems in your life, don't assume there is something wrong with you. Struggling with those problems is at the very core of life's purpose. As we draw closer to God, He will show us our weaknesses and through them make us wiser, stronger. If you're seeing more of your weaknesses, that just might mean you're moving nearer to God, not farther away" ("The Atonement: All for All," *Ensign*, May 2004, 97–98).

As part of repentance, suffering, and learning obedience, we must often "wait for a little season" (D&C 105:9) before blessings are restored and complete healing can take place. I suffered longer than I would have liked in mourning for my friend—but long enough to change.

Another difficult period in my life occcurred as I mourned for a lost relationship that I had hoped would result in marriage. My tendency was to pray for that relationship to be revived or to quickly find

a better one. Heavenly Father responded by granting me a prolonged season of loneliness and introspection, bringing many of my faults and mistakes into sharp focus. I'm grateful He offered me a time of humble preparation, no matter how painful, rather than the quick escape I was seeking.

After Zion's Camp failed in what they sought to accomplish, the Lord revealed that the Saints would benefit from waiting for Zion's redemption so that "they themselves may *be prepared*, and that my people may *be taught* more perfectly, and *have experience*, and *know more perfectly concerning their duty*, and the things which I require at their hands" (D&C 105:10, emphasis added). Like the early Saints, we often believe *in theory* what the Lord requires, yet still feel surprised when cutting corners does not bring the same blessings. We may fear the Lord does not love us because He will not overlook our disobedience and grant us the blessings we desire. May we learn to thank Him for not allowing us to settle for less than we can be! He is preparing and teaching us, not depriving us.

Waiting for blessings after we have transgressed is not a punishment as much as a sacred opportunity to learn the laws that govern happiness. The Lord understands that transgressions sometimes result from immaturity or inexperience rather than a blatant desire to sin. In His mercy, He does not spare us experience. He witholds some blessings until we've become equipped *through* our experience to utilize them for good.

Moving On

Because the opportunity to gain experience is a gift, we should accept it with gratitude, carrying valuable lessons forward—without forever carrying the guilt. Though carrying a heavy burden for a time can strengthen our spiritual muscles, carrying it longer than required brings fatigue, undermining the strength we could have gained and rendering us useless.

Elder Kenneth L. Higbee of the Seventy once explained, "Mistakes are not only an acceptable part of

life, but they may even be beneficial. The intelligent use of our mistakes helps us learn and grow; past failures may be guideposts to future successes. But our failures and mistakes can be constructive only if we analyze them, gain what profit we can from them, and then forget them" ("Forgetting Those Things which Are Behind," *Ensign*, Sept. 1972, 83).

Joseph Smith and Martin Harris were forgiven for losing the 116 pages. They left their sin behind them and went on to complete a great work: the Book of Mormon came forth, Joseph fulfilled his prophetic mission, and Martin Harris became one of the Three Witnesses to the divinity of the book.

President Boyd K. Packer of the Quorum of the Twelve Apostles said, "I do not think it pleases the Lord when we worry because we think we never do enough or that what we do is never good enough" ("The Least of These," *Ensign*, Nov. 2004, 87). The whisperings of the Spirit will tell us when we have suffered enough. We must plead to hear our Savior's voice and surrender our heavy load when He asks for it.

Returning Home

I've often thought about the parallel between the experiences of Zion's Camp and the transgression made in the garden of Eden. Just as Adam and Eve lost paradise in order to become sanctified in a mortal wilderness, the Saints were cast out of Jackson County—the former physical location of paradise, according to modern revelation—so they could gain strength by crossing a great American wilderness. Both Adam and Eve and the early Saints encountered wilderness in order to appreciate the peaceful sanctuary of home.

So must we. If experienced in all humility, mortality has a refining effect. Our human mistakes can produce holiness. Interestingly enough, the footnote attached to 2 Nephi 9:20 indicates that one meaning of "holy" is "committed." As we experience failures and challenges, may we become more committed to the Lord, more committed to His laws, and more committed to obedience. Then when we pass into the next world, we will arrive with the capacity

to obey the laws required to live in eternal happiness there.

Jesus Christ paid the price for us to "learn from [our] experience without being condemned by it," Elder Hafen taught. As long as we repent, we are not condemned for the errors in judgment, mistakes, and occasional sins that learning entails. We are not blamed for lacking the expertise only experience can bring. We must remember that "this earth is not our home. We are away at school, trying to master the lessons of 'the great plan of happiness' (Alma 42:8) so we can return home and *know what it means to be there*" (Bruce C. Hafen, *Ensign*, May 2004, 97–98).

As we rightfully accept the guilt and pain of sin, learn from our failings, and then, through the Atonement's miraculous power, let them go, we will change. We will accomplish the purpose of our mortal schooling and carry those lessons home into eternity.

Chapter 4

A Holy Sacrifice: When Failure Is Success

*J*ohn Griffiths is one of my ancestors. He left his home in England with his four children, two sons and two daughters. His young sons died on the journey and were buried in the snow. On November 30, 1856, John arrived in Salt Lake with his daughters, all of them nearly starved and frozen. The next day he died.

If the success of the Martin and Willie Handcart companies could be measured in black and white statistics, it could be argued that they suffered terrible failures. Many of their members died before achieving their goal of reaching Zion. Years later, a group sensed this tragedy and indulged in criticizing the

Church for having allowed the handcart pioneers to begin their trek so late in the season. Francis Webster had crossed the plains as a handcart pioneer at the age of 26 with his wife and baby. Now sitting in the back of the room, he arose to speak. "His face was white with emotion, yet he spoke calmly, deliberately, but with great earnestness and sincerity.

"He said in substance, . . .'You are discussing a matter you know nothing about. Cold historic facts mean nothing here for they give no proper interpretation of the questions involved. A mistake to send the handcart company out so late in the season? Yes. . . . But did you ever hear a survivor of that company utter a word of criticism? Not one of that company ever apostatized or left the Church because every one of us came through with the absolute knowledge that God lives for we became acquainted with him in our extremities" (Gordon B. Hinckley, "Our Mission of Saving," *Ensign*, Nov. 1991, 54).

Francis Webster understood success. The end goal that eluded hundreds of handcart pioneers was

secondary to what they accomplished instead—a profound spiritual victory. They remained true, their solid faith affecting generations. When I think of John Griffiths, I don't mourn his early death or the fact that he never enjoyed the peaceful life he sought amid the Saints. I celebrate the faith that propelled him across the plains. I thank him for bringing his righteous posterity to a place where they could build the Church and lay a foundation for blessings I enjoy. His sacrifices *were* the success.

Our Best Offerings

As we expend our sacred efforts, we too are successful in the Lord's eyes. Through scripture He tells us, "When I give a commandment to any of the sons of men to do a work unto my name, and those sons of men go with all their might and with all they have to perform that work, and cease not their diligence, and their enemies come upon them and hinder them from performing that work, behold, it behooveth me to require that work no more at the

hands of those sons of men, but to accept of their offerings" (D&C 124:49).

The Lord understands the nature and power of our enemies, whether they are other people; physical limitations imbedded in our corruptible, mortal bodies; emotional trials; or any number of weaknesses and uncontrollable barriers. Notice that the Lord accepts our best *offerings*, not just favorable results. The importance of success will weigh less on our minds as we savor opportunities to sacrifice.

John S. Tanner, a BYU humanities professor, said in a BYU convocation address: "A success culture values achievement rather than effort. The root meaning of *success* is 'result.' . . . [However] what endears us to heaven is our sincere sacrifice. . . The Almighty does not require success, but he does require sacrifice" ("On Sacrifices and Success," *BYU Magazine*, Fall 2003, 2). Elder M. Russell Ballard of the Quorum of the Twelve Apostles emphasized this requirement when he said: "If I have a fear, it is that the principle of sacrifice may be slipping away from us.

This principle is a law of God. We are obliged to understand it and practice it" ("The Law of Sacrifice," *Ensign*, Oct. 1998, 7).

We practice it by surrendering our will to Heavenly Father, regardless of whether He promises us the success we desire in return. May we recognize that our ability to surrender is the greatest success Heavenly Father desires for us.

Elder Henry B. Erying spoke of a time he sought heavenly guidance, knowing what choice looked most comfortable to him and what outcome he wanted. He says, "I prayed, but for hours there seemed to be no answer. Just before dawn, a feeling came over me. . . . I found myself praying, 'Heavenly Father, it doesn't matter what I want. I don't care anymore what I want. I only want that Thy will be done. That is all that I want. Please tell me what to do.'

"In that moment I felt as quiet inside as I had ever felt. And the message came, and I was sure who it was from. It was clear what I was to do. *I received no*

promise of the outcome. There was only the assurance that I was a child who had been told what path led to whatever He wanted for me" ("As a Child," *Ensign*, May 2006, 16, emphasis added).

The Doctrine and Covenants forever preserves the name of another man who was not guaranteed success when issued a command. President Boyd K. Packer tells us that Oliver Granger was "an ordinary man" who was "mostly blind." He was called to stay behind in Kirtland and try to sell the Saints' properties. President Packer said, "There was not much chance that he could succeed. And, really, he did not succeed!" ("The Least of These," *Ensign*, Nov. 2004, 86). Yet the Lord promised that Oliver's name "shall be had in sacred remembrance from generation to generation, forever and ever" (D&C 117:12). Oliver is praised, not because of what he achieved, but because of his obedience. The Lord says, "His sacrifice shall be more sacred unto me than his increase" (D&C 117:13).

More Sacred Than Increase

A few years ago a group of friends and I set out to raise funds to help a friend in need. Our friend's wife, Maggie, had died suddenly, leaving him with a pile of medical and funeral bills that threatened to sink his meager student budget. I felt inspired to organize a benefit concert despite the fact that I had no event planning experience whatsoever. In the two months leading up to the concert, I stressed over the fear that no one would come. I prayed about specific dollar amounts I hoped we could raise and pleaded with Heavenly Father that He would make our efforts successful.

The night of the concert arrived. It would have been Maggie's 25th birthday. As the musicians began singing, my heart sank. Less than 25% of the tickets had sold, and the city hall auditorium seemed achingly empty. I was happy to see so many of Maggie's friends and family, but we hadn't generated much support in the larger community.

I sat back, trying to resign myself to the possibility of a financial flop. I listened to the carefully chosen songs and let my eyes wander around the room. The walls were adorned with Maggie's artwork. I glanced back at the snack bar, manned by one of Maggie's old neighbors. I looked at the art prints a local painter had donated for us to sell, images of Maggie when she was a toddler. From the back row, I watched Maggie's loved ones dance, sing along, and quietly cry. Gradually the room became less empty as I recognized the immense love filling it.

By the end of the evening I was humbled. I knew that the Lord had inspired my group of friends to offer Maggie's loved ones something much more valuable than money. In my determination to pay for Maggie's funeral costs I had lost sight of any other good that could come from our sacrifices. The concert granted us the opportunity to celebrate her birthday in an uplifting tribute, creating memories and closer friendships more sacred than money.

I learned later that we had exceeded our fund-

raising goal. The few people who had attended were generous beyond measure. I was pleased, but the money didn't matter to me anymore. I had learned that our sacrifices given in service *were* the success, and that fact remained regardless of the material outcome.

The Savior's Image

Elder Ballard taught, "The word sacrifice means literally 'to make sacred'" ("The Law of Sacrifice," *Ensign*, Oct. 1998, 8). The Almighty requires only what we can control, meaning our efforts and our will. Sacrificing our will to obey the Father can bring some of the greatest psychological and emotional wrestling we will experience in mortality, but it makes us holier beings. Unfortunately, we often undervalue the very efforts that sanctify us and expect to achieve recognizable "increase."

As a long-time member of a singles ward, I caved into the discouraging standard of outward performance. I began wondering if my lack of success in dating was displeasing to the Lord because I was not

married. I measured my efforts only by the expectation that I should have achieved results by now! I felt inadequate and heartbroken until the Holy Ghost whispered a scripture to my mind: "Verily I say unto you, all among them who know their hearts are honest, and are broken, and their spirits contrite, and are willing to observe their covenants by sacrifice—yea, every sacrifice which I the Lord shall command—they are accepted of me.

"For I, the Lord, will cause them to bring forth as a very fruitful tree which is planted in a goodly land, by a pure stream, that yieldeth much precious fruit" (D&C 97:8–9).

I felt comforted by the image of a tree and the promise that, through my sacrifices, I could become fruitful. This promise rings of Messianic imagery, reminding me of another fruitful tree seen in vision by Lehi and Nephi.

Elder Holland cited 1 Nephi 11:7 when he taught that "the images of Christ" and the Tree of

Life are "inextricably linked" (*Christ and the New Covenant*, Deseret Book, 1997, 160). The Spirit explained to Nephi, "And behold this thing shall be given unto thee for a sign, that after thou hast beheld the tree which bore the fruit which thy father tasted, thou shalt also behold a man descending out of heaven, and him shall ye witness; and after ye have witnessed him ye shall bear record that it is the Son of God." The Tree of Life is a sign, or a symbol, of Jesus Christ. This explanation is repeated by Nephi in verse 25: "I . . . beheld that the tree of life was a representation of the love of God." We know that the greatest evidence of God's love is the Savior: "For God so loved the world, that he gave his only begotten Son" (John 3:16).

If the Tree of Life is a direct symbol of Christ and His mission, perhaps the tree in D&C 97 represents our opportunity to become like Him. As we sacrifice, He plants us next to a pure stream. We draw from the stream, nourishing our faith in the Savior. Alma tells us that such faith will "become a tree springing

up [in us] unto everlasting life" (Alma 33:23). We can become like Jesus Christ, abundant in all the eternal fruits that are "desirable to make one happy" (1 Nephi 8:10).

Sacrifice is the price we pay to draw from the stream, another symbol rich in meaning. Nephi tells us that the rod of iron led not only to the Tree of Life but also "to the fountain of living waters, . . . which waters are a representation of the love of God" (1 Nephi 11:25). Christ is the living water, and one of the places we immerse ourselves in this spiritually life-sustaining source is His temple. The Old Testament prophet Ezekiel prophesied of a temple in Jersusalem and recorded that "waters issued out from under the threshold of the house" (Ezekiel 47:1), growing into a river that healed and enlivened everything in its path (see vs. 8–9).

Our sincere sacrifices place us in the path of this living stream—our sacrifices to be worthy of entering the temple and to keep our temple covenants. On the other hand, seeking *only* worldly success at the

expense of humility and sacrifice may lure us toward another fountain seen by Nephi and Lehi, a "fountain of filthy water" (1 Nephi 12:16), "an awful gulf" (1 Nephi 15:28) representing all that the devil has to offer us—spiritual death, "misery and woe" (2 Nephi 1:13). As we sacrifice for the Lord, we will stay close to the living water and quietly grow. We will become genuinely fruitful in the things of the Spirit, not merely ornamental.

Rising Again

When we recognize that some deprivations are opportunities to sacrifice and we align our attitude accordingly, Heavenly Father will help our spirits "rise again." The Lord promised Oliver Granger, "When he falls, he shall rise again" (D&C 117:13). The promise, President Packer pointed out, is *when*—not if ("The Least of These," *Ensign*, Nov. 2004, 86). We are all given opportunities to fall so that we may adopt an attitude of willing sacrifice and rise to greater spiritual heights.

The Pearl of Great Price tells us: "And after many days an angel of the Lord appeared unto Adam, saying: Why dost thou offer sacrifices unto the Lord? And Adam said unto him: I know not, save the Lord commanded me" (Moses 5:6). Like Adam, we may not always see the reasons for the Lord's requirements at first.

I've seen this principle at work in the life of a dear friend following a disappointing end to his mission. He had consecrated great effort in becoming prepared and worthy to serve. He put his heart into his missionary service and agonized over poor health when illness forced him to return home six months early. He could have questioned, "Why must I sacrifice some of the best months of my life to cope with an illness?" He could have questioned his level of success because he had not met the regular standard of serving for the specified length of time. He didn't know all the reasons for his plight, only that the Lord—through priesthood blessings, personal revelation, and leaders' counsel—had commanded

him to come home. As he submitted in humility, the Savior's peace entered his life. He was granted missionary opportunities at home, and eventually he felt the Spirit confirming that the Lord had accepted his offering.

Only the Holy Ghost can impress upon each person when he or she has given an acceptable offering. Because Heavenly Father knows each of us deeply and individually, He requires different sacrifices fit to each person's needs and capacities. But one thing is common: our level of willingness to sacrifice *whatever the Lord commands* is of supreme importance.

A Winning Battle

Our willingness to labor for the Lord's cause counts for much even when failure seems inevitable. Surrounded by great wickedness and endless bloodshed, Mormon encouraged his son Moroni, "Let us labor diligently; for if we should cease to labor, we should be brought under condemnation; for we have a labor to perform whilst in this tabernacle of clay, that we may conquer

the enemy of all righteousness, and rest our souls in the kingdom of God" (Moroni 9:6). Mormon and Moroni knew the wickedness of their people. They realized that the Lord could not bless such a hard-hearted people with success, but they continued to fight for a private victory, the capacity to endure to the end. Our sacrifices help us "conquer the enemy of all righteousness" in the battlefield of our individual souls. We are spiritually strengthened by our sincere sacrifices, even when the battle seems lost on a larger scale.

I think of a young man who shuns immorality and the sins common to his peers, feeling discouraged that his example is ineffective to reverse the tide of evil around him. I think of the missionary who doesn't baptize anyone because his investigators are repeatedly poisoned by the influence of anti-Mormon literature. In such scenarios, these men see little success in their efforts, but the Lord sees the growth in their own spiritual stamina.

President Packer spoke in a modern parable of the

sacrifices—even seeming failures—Church members will undoubtedly face as we engage in the battle for our souls: "Imagine that you are attending a football game. The teams seem evenly matched. One team has been trained to follow the rules; the other, to do just the opposite. They are committed to cheat and disobey every rule of sportsmanlike conduct. . . .

"Soon the field is a quagmire. Players on both sides are being ground into the mud.

"The cheating of the opposing team turns to brutality. . . . It ceases to be a game and becomes a battle.

"Imagine that you confront the sponsor of the game and demand that he stop this useless, futile battle. . . . Has he no regard at all for the players?

"He calmly replies that he will not call the game. You are mistaken. There is a great purpose in it. You have not understood.

"He tells you that this is not a spectator sport—it is for the participants. It is for their sake that he permits

the game to continue. Great benefit may come to them because of the challenges they face.

"He points to players sitting on the bench, suited up, eager to enter the game. 'When each one of them has been in, when each has met the day for which he has prepared so long and trained so hard, then, and only then, will I call the game.'

"Until then, it may not matter which team seems to be ahead. The present score is really not crucial. . . . Whatever is happening to the team, each player will have his day.

"Those players on the team that keeps the rules will not be eternally disadvantaged by the appearance that their team somehow always seems to be losing.

"In the field of destiny, no team or player will be eternally disadvantaged because they keep the rules. They may be cornered or misused, even defeated for a time. But individual players on that team, regardless of what appears on the scoreboard, may already be victorious.

"Each player will have a test sufficient to his needs; how each responds is the test. When the game is finally over, you and they will see purpose in it all, may even express gratitude for having been on the field during the darkest part of the contest." ("The Mystery of Life," *Ensign*, Nov. 1983, 17–18)

Seeking the Sacred

We can shake off the influence of our ambition-saturated culture and remember that earth life is not designed to offer one unqualified success after another. We may not always feel that we are succeeding, even in righteous causes, but we can prayerfully discover if we are passing the mortal test. We can discover if we are willingly sacrificing whatever the Lord requires in order to become more like Him. From an eternal perspective, success and sacrifice are often the same.

Like Oliver Granger, we can expect to sometimes "fall"—or fail to achieve our own hopes and expectations. But if our hearts are humble, we can *always* meet Heavenly Father's merciful expectations.

I conclude this chapter with John S. Tanner's closing remarks: "The world will judge you mainly by outcomes, not by effort. Unlike God, humans possess no window to the soul. We are not privy to the obstacles each person must overcome nor to each person's unique portion of talents. In this fallen world, therefore, you must be prepared to be measured by your success because outcomes are often all that can be measured.

"But do not measure yourself by the world's imperfect standard! Remember that he who looks not on the countenance but on the heart (1 Samuel 16:7) sees beyond your resume. He sees your soul. He knows your sacrifices, and they are sacred to him" ("On Sacrifices and Success," *BYU Magazine*, Fall 2003, 4).

Chapter 5

Walking on Water: Success through the Son of God

The ship crashed through "the midst of the sea, tossed with waves: for the wind was contrary" (Matthew 14:24). Violent waves slammed against the boat. Frightened and weary, the disciples rowed for their lives. All the while Jesus looked on (see Mark 7:48). Then, when it seemed daylight would never come, somewhere between the hours of three and six o'clock in the morning, "Jesus went unto them, walking on the sea" (Matthew 14:25). Perhaps Peter heard his name riding on the wind. Through pelting rain, he and his brethren looked up to see Christ coming to their rescue. "And . . . they were troubled, saying, It is a spirit; and they

cried out for fear" (vs. 26). They shrank from their very source of help.

"But straightway Jesus spake unto them, saying, Be of good cheer; it is I; be not afraid.

"And Peter answered him and said, Lord, if it be thou, bid me come unto thee on the water.

"And he said, Come" (vs. 27–29).

To all of us the invitation is the same: "Come unto me. Learn of me. See what I do. *Do* what I do, and I will sustain you."

Peter accepted the invitation. With eyes riveted on his Redeemer, he took a few tremulous steps into the waves. Like the Son of God, he was walking on water—the second person in the history of the world ever to do so. But "when he saw the wind boisterous, he was afraid; and beginning to sink, he cried, saying, Lord, save me.

"And immediately Jesus stretched forth his hand, and caught him, and said unto him, O thou of little faith, wherefore didst thou doubt?" (vs. 30–31)

We often remember Peter's failure to keep his focus on the Lord; we remember his small amount of faith and his overpowering doubts. The same could be said of most of us as we take our first steps into the unknown—we have a *little* faith. We have enough faith to answer when the Lord calls, but we may not have enough faith to feel the assurance of what will follow. Trusting the outcome to God, we step out of the boat. We hope we will not sink and hear the Lord say, "O thou of little faith." We do not want to suffer the shame of failure in His sight.

On another occasion Jesus said, "If ye have faith as a grain of mustard seed, . . . nothing shall be impossible unto you" (Matthew 17:20). Perhaps the way Jesus identified Peter in this moment, one "of little faith," was not in the spirit of rebuke. Perhaps it was an encouragement, a reminder to Peter that he had faith in the Son of God, however small—even as small as a grain of mustard seed. With such little faith, Peter had *power*. With only a little amount of faith, all of it centered in the Savior, he defied nature. He took

his first steps on the waves toward his master like a toddler taking his first steps toward loving parents.

Peter did not anticipate the obstacles that would continue to torment him despite his momentous act of faith. Overwhelmed, he fell, like so many of us have done and will do again. Yet what parent would rebuke a child for stumbling as he takes his first steps? As Jesus Christ yearns to do for *all* of us, He stepped forward "immediately" (Matthew 14:31) and caused Peter to "rise again" (D&C 117:13).

When we remember Peter, may we recognize that of all the disciples caught in the storm, he exercised the *most* faith and enjoyed the *most* success, not the least. He was the only one to step out of the boat. Only he put the Savior's invitation to the test, personally discovering that what Jesus had done, he could do. Sustained by his faith for a few steps, Peter briefly practiced the focused kind of faith that would grow and solidify throughout his life. The other disciples witnessed Christ's power that night; Peter experienced it.

As mortals we develop our faith and our capacities line upon line. A few successful steps followed by a fall are hardly failure—experience carries us forward. As we cry for the Savior to rescue us, He will. He knows our level of faith, and He does not look away in disappointment at our weakness. As Elder Holland said, "Considering the incomprehensible cost of the Crucifixion, Christ is not going to turn His back on us now" (*Trusting Jesus*, Deseret Book, 2003, 67).

We need not avoid the Lord's gaze nor fear His help. Only He knows what we may become, and only He knows what is required for us to reach our ultimate potential. He guides us there by giving us educational stepping-stones, stretching our patience, requiring our repentance, and accepting our sacrifice. In the end, our successes are by and through Him, our failures swallowed up in the miracle of His Atonement.

Let us go forward into daylight, basking in the joy Christ radiates. May we leave our failures behind,

accepting instead the Savior's gifts—healing from our disappointments, refinement through our experiences, and His ultimate commendation, "Well done, thou good and faithful servant" (Matthew 25:21).